I've Been Working on the Railway

Bruce Roseberry

PublishAmerica
Baltimore

First printing

ISBN: 1-59286-604-2
PUBLISHED BY PUBLISHAMERICA, LLLP
www.publishamerica.com
Baltimore

Printed in the United States of America

Table of Contents

There is the right way
the wrong way
and the railway

Anonymous

I've Been Working on the Railway

Operating Ratio

called us all in today
room packed with laborious faces
and coffee refills
doughnuts absent

talked about the operating ratio
for every dollar earned
costs the company eighty cents
gotta to keep costs down
got me to thinking

took the plan home, discussing
over roast beef
and Yorkshire pudding
not enough cash flow coming in
too much going out
here on in…

worried voices charging at me
"what about the new mountain bike,
Nike roller blades, summer camps,
new dining room table?"
here on in…

kitchen table deserted
except for the plan and myself
sitting
between half-full supper plates
apple pie absent

Although cabooseless trains were in operation in some parts of the country in the late 1980s it was not until 1990 that all trains freight trains became cabooseless. Today, there are still some cabooses stored away in back tracks mainly used for work trains and local switching assignments.

FRED

for years an integral component
of every freight train
marker lights and conductor's grips
fresh coffee percolating
tuned generator motor pounding in sync
metal cabinets vibrating
kitchen cutlery dancing on the shelves

trainline hoses coupled
as the northerly wind whips across the tracks
piercing like a sharp knife
radiant heat from the oil stove
burning so quietly
thawing red faces and
frozen leather work boots
twenty minutes of refuge
while air reserviors sing to the charge

no more caboose
long gone are the days
sitting up in the cupola
idle conversations

escaping the elements
ridiculous delays
over axes and kitchen spatulas
checking for air flow
lightly tapping the gauge

technological advancement
replaced with end of train unit
the SBU—sense and brake unit
device attached to rear of train
displays and records trainline pressure
nicknamed FRED when first introduced
Effing Rear End Device…

Assignment 7116

Canadian Pacific Railway
owns 50,000 pieces of rolling stock equipment
Crestbrook Forest Industries
owns thirty-three
green log flats
operating on the Windermere Sub
Assignment 7116

Frozen Hoses and Running Noses

Winter Action Plans
and
Customer Demands

Non Stop Conference Calls
and
Alert Level WALS

Continuous 12-Hour Shifts
and
Warranty Service Agreements

Out of Round Wheels
and
Major Grain Spills

Snow-Covered Switches
and
Woolen Underwear Itches

Avalanche Control Zones
and
Out of Reach Cellular Phones

100 Series Trains
and
Perilous Freezing Rains

WILD Detectors
and

Blowin' Fuel Injectors

Christmas Vacation Shelved
and
Start up Plans to Meld

So Zip up the Fleeces
and
Bundle out the Cold

Face Those Arctic Freezes
and
Get the Damn Trains Over the Road

Setoff at Leanchoil

the Yoho breeze darts through
the towering fir trees
sending shivers among the
seasoned green pine needles

                                        undesired releases
                                        brake pipe rise

tree branches coming alive
swaying and drooping
to the gale wind force
transforming the sleeping snow
into a white cloud of wintry dust

                                        emergency feature
activated

                                        low air pressure
mushrooming particles of frozen vapor
falling lazily downward
the sound of ice granulars
lightly tap dancing
atop the metal hood
then gracefully bowing to liquid
from the heat of the idling truck motor

                                        downloaded information
                                        equalizing reservoir air
waiting comfortably
inside the warm climate controlled
Dodge truck cab
as the perplexed train crew
begrudgingly sets out the bad order car
constant calls from the rail traffic controller

how much longer?
westbound trains backed up

angle cocks cut in
brake valve cut out

five more minutes to proceed
from a two hour train delay
to the late night office reports
explaining basic air brakes "101"
creatively

The Day Hollywood Came

Yardmaster like a town cryer
bellowed out the tidings
scenes from a movie now being filmed
northend of the train yard
I guess that explains
why all of those white mobile trailers
all at once appeared out of nowhere

makeup artists to accentuate
Allie McPherson's beauty
Anthony Hopkins' blue eyes
Alec Baldwin's boyish grin
and of course the main star
all 1,000 lbs with brown matted fur
Bart the grizzly bear

looming in the background
in full view of the film cameras
are the stored old CP woodchip cars
but for now they have to be relocated
and replaced with leased DLRX lumber cars
for these rail cars provide the realism
that transforms the filming site
from British Columbia Canada
to a makeshift Alaska USA

Edward Mallandaine was only 17 years young when he pushed his way into Canada's most famous
railway photo.

Craigellachi—The Last Spike

the damp air tingled with anticipated excitement
groups of men gathered together
on that early November day back in 1885
disconcerned over the low lying grey somber skies
history was in the making
the contemporary box camera poised
photographer's head covered in a state of preparedness
positioned to record forever this historical event

young Edward Mallandaine stands
in front of a group of distinguished bearded men
unaware of the real significance of this photo
his right foot firmly planted on the rail
peering his boyish face
into the pages of Canadiana
witnessing Lord Strathcona pounding the last spike
completing the railroad and
binding together the Dominion of Canada
with the hands of steel now reaching
from the Atlantic to the Pacific

Pierre Burton eventually dubbed it
"Canada's National Dream"
uniting and strengthening this great land

strange how this nostalgic railway
with its beaver logo
has lent itself during the past century
to so many photos, stories and songs

gone are the long white beards and black top hats
replaced by clean-shaven and well-manicured MBA executives
dressed in Dockers and two-piece skirt suits
holed up inside glass-walled fish bowl conference rooms
strategizing and planning
the once abundant magnitude of east west traffic
now being challenged by the population based US markets
with the changing traffic trend
the question now commonly posed
is it sea to shining sea?
or sea to Gulf of Mexico?

Short Line

Carolina Costal Railway is a tiny line
at least
compared to the multi-thousand-mile systems
its tracks span a mere seventeen miles
the entire railroad has only two employees
who
on alternate days
either run trains
or perform track and equipment maintenance

25 Year Recognition Award

a time for reflection
that first day
twenty-five years ago

accomplishment in its own right
asked me if I wanted a presentation

a temporary placement
only here for a short while
like a passing sun shower
I too will move on

engraved pendulum clocks
beaver emblemed rings
please—no bells, no parades
just my gift

summers turned to winters
winters to years
faces forever etched
careers fading into the twilight

a forever keepsake
worn for personal fulfillment
colored with emotion
silently displayed for all to view

over coffee rows
and supermarket checkouts
with all its gleam
adoring admiration
stirring conversations

"nice ring" commonly echoed
"yeah—25 years"

who would have thought

Safety

five minute safety talks
job briefings
safety reps
watch your step

safety meetings
committee sittings
site inspections
make no exceptions

safety action plans
safety audits
safety stats
safety hats

safety concerns
job procedures
safety awareness
don't be careless

safety commitment
safe environment
one to ones
and try to get some work done

Nightly Visitor

scrambling into the confined safety
of the locomotive cab
slamming the steel doors shut
heart pounding to a thousand beats
steady on the horn
HONNNNNK HONNNNK

down below
the black bear
wades through the dumpster's spoils
his quest for food scraps
rudely interrupted
by the deafening horn blasts
HONNNNNK HONNNNNK

eyes fixated upon each other
with an unblinking stare
my face showing shear fright
the end of his nose showing
remnants of a tuna salad sandwich
HONNNNNK HONNNNNK

yardmaster over the radio
ENOUGH OF THE HORN
IT'S THREE A.M.
YOU'LL WAKE UP THE WHOLE TOWN

easy for you to say
come on out here
and you service these locomotives

without ending up as the daily entree
I have to try and scare this bear away
HONNNNNK HONNNNNK

all the while
sleeping comfortably at home
the afternoon shift switchman
unaware of the problems of
placing food scraps by dumpster
every day
HONNNNNK HONNNNNK

Pecking Order

Four levels of management
all sharing the same taxi
full sized yet limited
the late night jet lag
dampening any meaningful conversation

airport to home
directional one-way traffic flowing
to a convoy of red tail lights
headlight and streetlight glare
reflecting down through
the rain-slicked intersections

drop-offs
starting from the top level
from the most affluent area
continuing on
to the downtown pricy high rise townhouses
motoring on through the city
meter never missing a beat

finally, modest suburbia
last stop
time to find my keys
gather my bags
and pay the hundred-dollar cab fare

Idle Hands

computers are down again
like a power blackout
a deafening cyberspace silence
descends over the keyboard
interrupted only by the
ringing tone of the desk phone
an audible so loud
so energetic
a welcome relief
to this lasting idleness

all the while
daily reports expected
correspondence on pause
time verifications not approved
payroll accuracy in limbo
and solitaire
waiting to be conquered

Orson Welles once said there are two emotions on an airplane—boredom and terror, thank God most people will only ever experience boredom.

Valentine's Day

two plus hours of
monotonous air travel time to pass
cabin lights dimmed
as laptops and magazines
appear out of hiding
aisle sandwich carts expeditiously propelled by
bronzed nyloned legged flight attendants

returning home after
time zones hotel rooms and boarding passes
inspecting new freight cars
at the assembly plant
interpreting engineering drawings
while industry suppliers and inspectors
amid distinctive drawl accents
swap business cards and presidential jokes

descending from 35,000 feet
with gaping yawns and popping ear drums
compiling Customs declaration forms
claiming
romantic gifts from America's heartland
heart-shaped chocolates
duty-free perfume
and a liter bottle of Weisers Deluxe

Banff

Trans Canada highway in the summertime
the continual stream of campers and vans
unfamiliar license plates with sayings
"show me state"
"empire state"
"peace garden state"
attentive eyes on the road
quick glances downward
to the marvel of
trains snaking steadily through the canyon
tracking alongside
the rushing white river waters
over bridges
through mountain black holes
curve for curve
looking like a gigantic HO model train set

lumber loads and orange double stacks
side by side at Ottertail
long line of empty sulphur cars
waiting at the crew changeout point
loaded grain train slowly
ESSing down the Field hill
navy blue passenger coaches
looking so orderly and refined
politely entering the Spiral tunnel
dome observation cars
swelling with binocular strapped tourists

driving into Banff
sold out Eric Harvie theater
Earls at midnight
Old Spaghetti Factory at lunch
browsing, shopping
leap frogging under the shop canopies
dodging the cool wet downpour
spellbound from the magical aroma
of the Yuletide store
elk in the park
elk in the town
elk droppings in my pocket
chocolate of course

back on the highway
jockeying for position
road construction and slow orders
passing lanes and clear boards
start to finish
twenty-four hours in Banff

What Did You Do on the Railroad?

pounded 100,00 track spikes
changed 50,00 brake shoes (cursed most of them)
threw 10,000 track switches
unloaded 100,000 wheelsets
changed out 10,000 of those wheelsets
rerailed 1000 cars
fueled 25,000 locomotives
went up and down the 32 step shop stairwell 40,000 times
received over 800 pay cheques
attended 300 safety meetings
wore out 26 pair of safety boots
never experienced a reportable ranking injury
issued 120 demerits
received demerits on three occasions
filed four grievances
late for work 14 times

Wrecking

Subject to Change

Through the dark of night
we fumble in and around
the twisted metal
trying to fathom
some form of semblance
to this temporary chaos

Knowing very well
the morning light
will greet us with an arrogant sneer
showing all a different perspective

The formulated plan of action
agreed upon
over six volt flashlights
will now have to be altered
has to be that way
subject to change
it always is

The first spiral tunnel mishap occurred on April 18, 1994, the exact cause can still to this day be debated. New steel railway track ties were installed shortly after the derailment cleanup was completed.

Six Days

Six days in the tunnel and
I'm going to make it home tonight

Fifteen loaded potash cars to rerail
Room in the tunnel to no avail
Worked in shifts around the clock
Pressure is on with the mainline blocked

Six days in the tunnel and
I'm going to make it home tonight

Nine cars had to transfer their load
The opening of the track was put on hold
Air quality caused us all to beware
Huge fans were brought in to circulate the air

Six days in the tunnel and
I'm going to make it home tonight

Darkness in the tunnel was a constant night
Most valuable tool was a dependable light
Transferring the loads was quite a chore
Noise of the machines was a continuous roar

Six days in the tunnel and
I'm going to make it home tonight

It was a tough road to hoe
At times progress was ever so slow
Our efforts would not be curtailed
One by one the cars were emptied and rerailed

Six days in the tunnel and
I'm going to make it home tonight

Auxiliary Breakfast

the pettibone mobile crane hirailed passed us
moving at an alarming speed
the hirail wheels barely clinging
to the frail fragile looking
eighty-five pound rails
wooden ties sinking and rising
under the weight
of this versatile machine
visible for miles with its
bright reddish yellow markings

all of us staring in bewilderment
where are they going?
there are still five mishap hopper cars
lying on their sides
string lined beside the track
waiting to be uprighted

the mobile crane shoots past the lift site
past the hardwood blocks and half ties
neatly stacked from the previous day
as its wheels skid to an abrupt stop
all three crew members bail out
with panic-stricken faces
and tissue in hand
they dash for cover

our crane is blocked
ready to make a lift
steel wire cables wrapped tightly

as they prepare their crane
over freshly dug blocking indentations
the operator walks over to me
“what did the cook put in the eggs?”
“nothing, we all had breakfast at the auxiliary diner”
“you tell your cook I’ll get even”
“honest, we all ate the same breakfast”
“B.S., all three of us at one once
something must have been added”
“no, our cooks would never do that…
must have been the coffee”

as he walked back to his crane
I could still hearing him muttering
about the cooks and getting even
his pockets brimming with rolls
of white toilet paper

Hurry Up and Wait

Called six o'clock for seven
stacks of blueberry pancakes
and endless cups of coffee
unshaven faces showing signs of fatigue
attired in their work suits
navy colored coveralls and bright orange hardhats
with picnic coolers in tow
they board the idler
well stocked with drinking water, sodas, juices and power drinks
the required nourishment
for these 90 degree plus sweltering days
the heavy air hazy from the recent rash of forest fires

A solemn oath to get us on the track
possibly six hours of recovering derailed equipment
the early morning coolness
like a breath of fresh air
A welcome relief from the stifling unbearable hot afternoon sun
train clearances, authorities and work betweens
the never ending series of radio conversations, acknowledgements & repeats
railroad red tape
burning up our precious track time
do they not realize cranes have to be blocked
heavy wire cables wrestled into position
bent and broken couplers replaced

here we sit waiting—patiently…
someone asks what day is it
I have to stop and think…

someone asks what time is it
I dare not look at my watch…
knowing very well the minute hand keeps ticking away
reducing our track time considerably
resulting in yet another day set back
the best laid plans
and still haven’t turned a wheel
hurry up and wait…

Flagman at Mileage 24.5

Two 400 series expedited trains sideswiped
overturning three locomotives
flopping them on their sides against the sun-baked earth
the echoing sound of 12,000 tons colliding
bringing some unexpected excitement
to this otherwise desolate desert like countryside
the late afternoon blistering August sun
bearing witness to the entire chain of events

lightweight metal merchandise containers
sheared and torn wide open
contents scattered over the covering sagebrush
sporting goods computers
school supplies cameras
books and clothing
in a split second
the ground instantly transformed into
a cardboard box landfill

I came upon some of our crew
huddled in a small group
laughing joking inflating
what I thought to be rubber dingies
first an arm shot out
then a leg
HEY! these aren't rubber dingies
they are inflatable dolls
companions for John Does
sexual…whatevers

vibrators, blow up dolls, love potions
spoils form the Love Shop

CP Police were quickly on the scene
the area was corded off
with eagle eye surveillance
every square inch inspected
all of the merchandise was commandeered
damaged or not

I eventually asked our crew
did we take anything?
no, not us boss

five days later
the area fully restored
slow train orders removed
returning home riding our auxiliary train
standing on the walkway catching some scenery
the warm sensation of hot dry air
permeating my clean shaven face
tender from the recent removal of
a six-day-old poor facsimile of a beard
when I noticed a flagman up ahead
at mileage 24.5
as we approached it became apparent
this is no flagman
it is one of the blow up dolls
a brunette fully inflated
green flag taped to its hand
the warm breeze
causing the doll to gently rock back and forth

Old and the New

thirty-year-old leased
delapitated steel coal cars
rattling down the track
wheels thumping to the beat
of broken side sheet welds
grinning from coupler to coupler
as they slowly pass by the derailment site

past the grossly disfigured
new aluminum coal cars
casualties from the impact
barely off the assembly line
now nothing more than scrap metal

CP 5660

The barges delivered the three locomotives
to the selected drop-off site on the shoreline
the auxiliary cranes spotted thirty feet above
their long sleek black booms
overlooking the calm looking water
center outriggers fully extended and blocked
the final stage of the recovery process

submerged in 70 feet of darkness
for the last five months
a wintry rock slide without any forewarning
halted the west bound dead in its tracks
toppling the three locomotives
down the sharp inclined bank
into the frigid depths of Kootenay lake
divers had to recover the bodies
trapped inside the locomotive cab
a two-hundred-ton steel coffin

two of the locomotives have already been lifted
put on dummy trucks
here comes the final one
the leader—CP 5660
this is the one where the two crew members
met their untimely death
with careers only half way completed
children's graduations never to attend
vacation plans
waiting to be digested over the supper table

wire rope cables resembling huge anacondas
tighten and stretch
hoisting the locomotive up to the track
lifting capacities and radius
precisely factored in to the equation
correct measurements taken

there is a strange aura
surrounding the locomotive
as the water corroded chassis
is gently lowered to the rails
an eerie feeling descends upon all of us
a stillness in the air
everyone is quiet
thoughts suspended in tranquility
thinking of the deceased crew
observing a moment's silence

Run Through Switch

keep forgetting
about that damn hardhat rain guard rim
every time I bend my neck forward
rain accumulation runs down
soaking my notebook
turning the written notes
into ink blotches
looks like it's going to rain all night

Date and Time
Yard Mileage
Run Through Switch Number
Point of Derailment

have to be a magician
flashlight in one hand
pen in the other
notebook resting on the cross over step
steady rain drizzle
my shorthand like notes
becoming more and more eligible
pen nib tearing the damp paper
MCB 23'Ds—damaged car reports

Car initials and numbers
Wheels derailed
"A" end R&L
"B" end R&L
Blt date

overcast, dreary, gloomy
and WET
cotton gloves soaked through
hands numb from the damp coldness
skin starting to wrinkle
the continual humming sound
of the rain landing on the ballast
like a muffled roar
if you think about it long enough
it will drive you crazy

Frame braces bent B end
Adapter out of place R-1
Truck Springs missing BR

replacers are clamped and wedged
2300 yard crew on route
1600 crew gone home—lucky ducks
four of the six loaded cars left to rerail
shouldn't take more than a couple of hours
then back home
dry clothes and a warm bed

Work Extra 6006

the crane and work train consist
wind itself around the lake
moving slowly yet steadily
through the early morning fog
approaching the derailment site
the 250-ton Brownhoist crane
resembling a giant preying mantis
with a 40-foot track panel
hanging down from its mouth
swinging ever so gently

CP Work Extra 6006
20 cars to a spot

it is quiet now compared
to only a few hours ago
D-9 cats and excavators
moving back and forth
pushing, pulling, ripping
their tracks leveling
everything in their path
turrets rotating 360 degrees

CP Work Extra 6006
10 cars to a spot

twenty loaded coal cars
most on their side
others upright positioned 90 degrees
across from where the twisted 136 lb rail

only yesterday was so intact and uniform
it made a track supervisor proud
that was yesterday
before CP 9581 west hauling
114 loaded coal cars derailed
causing a 30-hour delay to an
already congested mainline
no chance to re-route traffic here

CP Work Extra 6006
05 cars to a spot

all of the derailed cars
have now been cleared
road bed has been graded
time to lay track panels
400' of track tore up
11 track panels will be suffice

CP Work Extra 6006
02cars to a spot

half of the crew have gone to bed
got the call right before their shift
at the shop had ended
been up for 30 hours straight
working through the dark
wading through spilt coal
slinging cables and clevises
always fearful for the movement
of the cats and excavators

CP Work Extra 6006
OK to stop

An Old Friend

the sleeper car
always welcoming me
like a lifelong friend
even with my coveralls
covered with grain and coal dust
workboots soiled

we've been together forever
shared the seasons
understand each other's
moans and groans

my own retreat
the calm after the storm
night air unruffled
like camping out among the pines

sleeper lounge lit dimly
paperwork waiting patiently
base radio turned low
distant voices
guiding distant trains

25 MPH

approaching the witching hour
the homeward bound auxiliary train
rattles and creaks
through the crisp January stillness
the dark sky littered
with a thousand sparkling diamonds
one by one the composed crew
after calculating bank time from overtime
retire to their bunks
succumbing to weariness and
warm grey woolen blankets

walking through to the diner
deserted yet still serving stale overbrewed coffee
between cars
stepping awaringly over the metal grating walkway
a blast of harsh winter freshness
the sound of steel wheels on steel
clack clack clack clack clack
through the siding
the momentary slack action
coupler heads butting together
then stretching
pulling violently
as evident by the tables spilling their contents
and slumberless grumblings

through the switch and back on the main
meanwhile million dollar high merchandise traffic
and 16,000-ton heavy haul commodity trains

crewed up and moving
our 25 mph restricted work train
only hours ago receiving praise
now being cursed for all its handicap
from a high priority auxiliary train
to a least desirable pain in the ass train
contending for track occupancy
on this night

Feeding Time

the dark long boomed crane
resembling a fire breathing dragon
head nodding up and down
smoke flaring from its nostrils
poised, scanning the dead carcasses
in hibernation
for the last six months
now fully awake, hungry

down below
army ants wearing
reflectorized hats and vests
with shovels and hundred foot tape measures
scurrying back and forth
among the broken twisted bodies
steel bellies ripped open
their contents flowing
into a desert of red fertilizer

slowly the make believe creature
lowers its head
down towards the carnage
steel cables
drooling from its mouth
grabbing the first offering

over and over
the same procedure is repeated
until all of the maimed remains
have been disposed of

Runaway Train

December 02, 1997 the unthinkable happened
Grain train powered by two GE AC 4400 locomotives
pulling 11,000 tons
over 5,000 feet in length
speeding uncontrollably down a 2.2 percent grade
with no brakes to slow their descend

Reaching speeds up to 50 mph
on normal 15 mph track
the rail traffic controller for the Mountain Sub
doing her best to warn track people in the vicinity
"GET OFF THE TRACK"
literally yelling over the air waves
"PROTECT THE CROSSINGS in FIELD B.C.
WE HAVE A RUNAWAY TRAIN"
an audio voice so loud
yet so helpless to the situation

In the upper spiral tunnel at mileage 129.0
out of control at a speed of 46 mph
with freight car wheels exerting
excessive lateral forces
against the arc curved rails
29 cars separated from the train
13 of which derailed in the tunnel
cars jammed in so tight
it would take a panzer division
of side boom cats
and half a fortnight to free them

The train then continued uncontrolled
speeding excessively
mile posts becoming blurs
brakes in emergency
panicking train crew faces
turning white as the rocky mountain snow

Five miles later at mileage 134.4
the avoidance could no longer continue
the remaining 55 cars separated
50 of which derailed
majority slid down the bank
the crisp still air
interrupted by the thunderous ovation
of hundred ton metal toboggans
plowing down a two hundred foot embankment

By the grace of god
the locomotives remained intact
wheels firmly perched on the
bluish metal ribbons of steel
the engineer recovered the Dynamic Brake function
managed to stop at the Field Station
all that remained apart from the locomotives
was a coupler from the leading grain car
a lone survivor
still coupled to the trailing locomotive

When the grain dust and
overcast cloud inversion had cleared
a total of 2,500 feet of track was destroyed
64 of the 66 derailed cars were scrapped

10,200 tons of grain was spilled
9,000 tons was eventually recovered
took a week to re-open the mainline
15 days total for the cleanup
all hoping they would be home for Christmas

Shop & Train Yard

Old Roundhouse

floor covered with droppings
from feathered coo-ers
perched up on top
of old steam pipes
wooden boards covering
broken glass window frames
where sun rays once pierced
roof eroded to a sieve
allowing the seasonal drip
of rain and snow melting

haunted by images
of steamers and
men wearing fedoras
crawling under, on, over
these iron horses
checking boiler pressure
thirty-inch stroke cylinders
polishing and gleaming

abandoned work areas
inactive for years
gone are the machinists
with their hammers and pipe wrenches
adjusting main steam valves
connecting wheel coupling rods
replaced only by the memories
and stagnate water
lying motionless
in the sunken work pits

Periodically one who normally works the day shift will attend midnight shift safety meetings.

Midnight Safety Meeting

wiping sleep from
weary half shut eyes
last month's meeting minutes
strategically placed
around the table
vacant chairs waiting
for members and guests
representing all three shifts

some starting their shift
some ending
some daydreaming
of home in the sanctuary
one's own bed
lying next to
a warm soft body
partially covered
in La Senza
sensual touch of bare legs
enticing
arousing

around the table
old and new business
safety flashes and injuries
stale black coffee

and attache cases
taking on the look of
pizzas all dressed

Lac La Turd

surrounded by the authoritative
dull grey metal frost fence
a statement for all to heed
KEEP OUT
of these uninviting
green algae-covered waters

officially the town sewage plant
comedically renamed
"Lac La Turd"
as the makeshift sign reads

with the airport located
within a stone's throw
it occurred on an otherwise
uneventful routine Sunday
an ultralight homemade single seater plane
destined to Vancouver
crash landed in the middle
of this gelatinous thick body of water

the skeleton staff on shift
received the call, odd as it was
utilizing the shop mobile crane
with its 10-ton test line
they went fishing for the pilot and wreckage
reeling in the sole disconcerted flyer
who by now resembled the creature from the deep
it was off to the hospital reluctantly
the prognosis was deemed OK

however the physician on call
did prescribe a hot sterilizing shower
and a change of clothes
next day
looking a tad more presentable
this grounded air navigator
stopped by the shop and
thanked all for their assistance
heading back home
with a broken plane and broken ego
back to the drawing board
back to his unimpressed wife
and just when he thought
he was out of deep s_ _ _

The epitome of detecting a bad order while performing a train inspection—a car inspector's ultimate find.

Cracked Wheel

I've always wanted to find a cracked wheel
the steel plate staring at me
exposing itself with all its flaw
a freak of cast steel
born from the process of pouring
red-hot molten metal
flowing like volcanic lava
filling the pre-cast forms
cooling and hardening to the design
of round wheel plates and
cigar-shaped axles

started as a hairline crack
now a full-fledged break
sunlight shining through the separation
running the entire wheel diameter
up and over the flange
across the tread
down the rim
may travel another mile
ten miles
hundred miles
until that fateful second
shattering into the fast flowing air
a catastrophic failure with devastating results

for now it sits quietly under
the shade of the freight car
one of many in the steady parade of
three hundred and sixty degree shapes
only this one is different
waiting to be inspected
detected, removed from service
photographed and reported
post mortem at the Engineering Test department
autopsy results telling of casting inclusions

they will tell me it was a fantastic find
prevented a million-dollar derailment
possibly may have even saved a life
atta boy for myself
beaming with self-satisfaction
just doing my job
inspecting freight cars
day in and day out
yep,
I've always wanted to find a cracked wheel

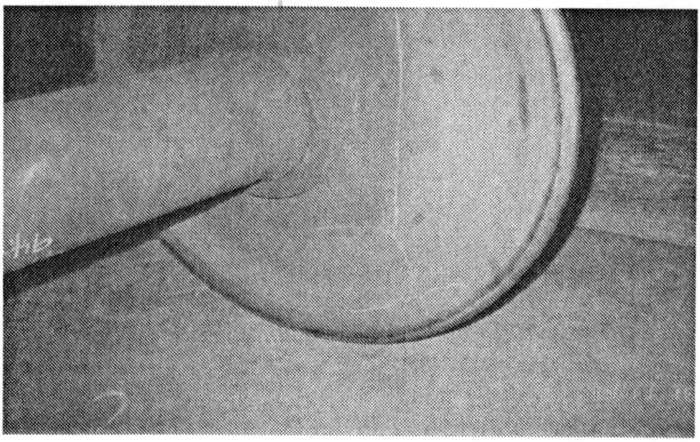

The Well-Trained Mechanic

books, handouts and a passing grade
lockout/blueflags and first aid
trade theory, car certification and WHIMIS
welding/torch and attitude awareness

ergonomics and hearing protection
fall arrest harnesses and CIM corrections
computers—merlin and SAP
dangerous goods and fire safety

trackmobiles, forklifts and cranes
heavy axle loaded trains
confined space and respirators
defensive driving plus air precipitators

slack adjusters, open top loads
AAR rules and billable codes
enviro barrels, solvents draining
human rights and harassment training

engine attendant recertification
optional food preparation
locomotives—GM and GE
downloads for all to see

The Puffer Belly Express train was built by a carman working out of the Golden car shop utilizing a Kabota tractor and lots of ingenuity. Built originally for local parades and school fun days, the train is now loaded on a flat car and travels throughout B.C. and Alberta attending railroad and municipal family functions.

Puffer Belly Express

The little train that could

All aboard!
children of all ages
painted faces, freckles
pony tails and pig tails
smiles highlighting missing baby teeth
patiently sitting, waiting
wooden coal and lumber car full
caboose bursting at the seams
arms and legs tucked in

ball peen hammer
clangs against the bell
throttle engages
black diesel smoke
bellows upwards
spiraling towards the sky

disguised as a steamer
the diminutive tractor
lurches forward

arousing exited cheers
faster, faster
echo the older children

chugging around the park
to the sweet aroma of cotton candy
waving to the fish pond anglers
sack race contestants
past the dunk tank tossers

back to the waiting parents,
the next batch of passengers
eagerly waiting their turn
to the same questions
can I sit in the caboose?
can I sit next to you?

Riptrack Romance

university students with
tuition fees and school loans
hired for the summer
Girls, all of them
personalities bubbling
excited yet cautious
workplace novelty
for eternity a male profession
fueling, watering, cleaning and supplying cabooses
van shack feminized
curtains hung ever so neatly
air tingling from the faint odor of perfume
railroad conductors apprehensive
carman apprentices inquisitive

their bond was immediate
both students in their own right
so much in common
hardhats, safety boots
coveralls, time cards
comparing pension contributions
union due deductions
drawn together over
broken copper water lines
time clock lineups
parking lot encounters

joined the softball team together
extra innings played out
at the local tavern

foozball table partners
flirting with uncertainty

summer faded into memories
attention turned to
dormitories and profs
journeyman status and night shifts
correspondence courting
weekend seminars

twenty years after
the van checker and the apprentice

Brake Cylinder Adjustment

125 shiny new aluminum coal cars to inspect
we've had our job briefing
armed with 3/4" and 1" wrenches
our mission
is to manually adjust the brake cylinders
it's going to be awkward trying
to fit around and under the trucks
loosening and tightening those spherical nuts

normally four go to the yard
this special assignment calls for eight
the middle of May
and it's raining with wet snow
forced to the train yard
away from the confines of the
warm dry shop comfort
coveted seniority or in this case lack of
forces me to the train yard

just my unfortunate luck
the four senior inspectors
have to leave to inspect another train
we've barely even started—maybe 10 cars adjusted
tightening the nut 3/8"
allows for 3/4" piston adjustment
I hope I got this right

on to the next car
these cars are brand spanking new
you would think they would be OK

not so
every trainset we lease
always requires some modification
why should these cars be any different

almost finishing and the sun is shining
the ordeal is over
the whining but a memory
last car to do—back to the shop
hamburgers are being grilled
it is employee appreciation day

In 1901 the collective agreement consisted of one entire page, today the agreement stretches 300 pages.

Collective Agreement Effective Oct 01, 1901

Article 1

Section 1— The regular hours worked shall be from 0700 to 1800 for the first five days and 0700 to 1700 for the sixth day.

Section 2 — Employees shall take their regular turn on night work.

Article 2

Section 1 — Any boy engaging himself as an apprentice to the carpenter's trade must be between the ages of 14 and 18; must be able to read and write and know the first four rules of arithmetic. Apprentices must serve at least 5 years, 300 working days to constitute a year.

Section 4 — Apprentices under the age of 18 years, who do not desire to work regular overtime or night shifts, must apply to the Foreman for relief.

Article 3

Section 1 — Wrecking crews will be paid straight time for traveling to and from wrecks and time and one-half while working at wrecks; no time to be allowed when laid up for rest.

Section 2 — When men are sent out on the road to work they will be allowed 75 cents per day for board.

Article 4

— When reductions in the force are necessary, men who have others dependent upon them for
support shall be given preference of employment.

Article VIII

Rates of pay:
Car Inspectors and Chargemen..................19 c to 21 1/2 c per hour
Air Brake Testers and Cleaners..................17 1/2 c to 20 c per hour
Track Repairers...17 1/2 c to 20 c per hour
Freight car Repairers..................................15 1/2 c to 18 c per hour
Car Oilers..15 1/2 c to 18 c per hour
Car Heating & lamp Men.........................15 1/2 c to 16 c per hour
Car Cleaners and Washers.........................13 1/2 c to 15 1/2 c per hour
Coach Carpenters..................................23 c to 26 c per hour
Coach Painters......................................20 c to 22 c per hour
Freight Car Painters..............................15 c to 20 c per hour

Last Day

trains arrive and depart
today just like yesterday
thirty-five years ago
steel wheels on steel rails
worn black composite brake shoes
squealing to be changed out
hissing of air exhausting through
hard rubber gaskets
soap bubbles ballooning and collapsing
around worn pipe fittings
all of these will be no more
for this day is not general to the
previous ten thousand days
only here is it so meaningful,
so special
inevitably his last day has arrived
the long trek now completed

was going to wait until
the trees colored amber
fallen leaves blanketing a career
filled with air brakes,
dump valves, snow plows
replacers, and couplers
Christmas came early this year
with a monetary package and pension
so neatly gift wrapped
it brought an ear-to-ear grin
to this Winston Churchill look-alike

harboring mixed emotions
rejoicing his retirement
mourning his departure
no more discussing air brakes
agonizing over the Leafs
penciling in Sunday gridiron picks
reminiscing over ice cold mugs in the Legion
of youthful recollections of dry warm air
blowing indiscreetly
across golden wheat fields

eventually all railroaders pull the pin
even the great ones
these old generation car knockers
work ethic from another era
train whistles will continue to blow
lunchboxes packed
defective wheelsets to renew
someone always fills the void
like removing your hands
from inside a pail full of water
the imprint quickly dissipates

all his gifts now collected
hands weary from farewell shakes
walking home for the last time
I got to stop him
say my final good-bye
relinquished to the fact
a part of me goes with him

The shop truck is predominately required to attend to locomotive problems and or concerns in the train servicing yard. Driven by numerous supervisors, the scenario can on occasion lend itself to having the truck being left from one shift another with little or no fuel remaining in the tanks.

Frustration

the fuel gauge reads E
both truck tanks parched
impacting train delays
possible emergencies
totally irresponsible

beseeched with anger
return to the office
message to all
"now hear this
now hear this"
keyboard being pounded
taking the blunt
frustration overboiling
like an overheated radiator

"how to fuel the truck"
simpletons,
I'll get even
step by step instructions
in sequential order

1—"open the gas tank cap"
2—"insert nozzle"
3—"begin fueling"
fingers moving rapidly
home the cursor
next line
satisfaction looming
blood temperature lowering
easy tiger, easy does it

4—"complete fueling"
5—"return nozzle"
6—"gas cap applied"

Now is that so hard
cool as a cucumber

First Shift

two newly hired employees
green as inexperience can be
huddled together
under the shop track's shimmering lights
choreographing their trembling bodies
to movement of an ancient tribal dance
desperately trying to fend off the cold

wishing their training orientation
could have lasted forever, or
until spring came to this frozen rail yard
a Siberian nightmare
the warmth of the office
but a distant memory

bundled in safety apparel
and thrown to the winter elements
200-ton power trembling locomotives
thirsty for fuel
unsympathetic to these greenhorn's plight

ill clad for working out in the elements
flashbacks to the college classroom
with warm thoughts of co-eds in tight sweaters
only to be overpowered
by the grim parental reminders
should have stayed in school
should have stayed in school

reality of working for a living
with minus thirty degree temperatures
first shift
a grave yard shift no less
and even the wind
shows no pity

The Glove Game

they were twin brothers
but you would never know it in appearance
only their heavy accents gave them away
worked the track for
thirty years and counting
know every inch of rail
from Field to Rogers

always coming to our shop
for welding jobs and
coincidently to see
what they can bum on the side
me anda mya crew needa gloves
can't you requisition your own?
what a matta?
nothing, you have to supply your own
what a matta with you?
nothing is the matter with me
you work for another department
what a matta witha youra department?
NOTHING!!!!!

conversation going nowhere
changing the subject
how is the track these days?
what a matta witha track?
I don't know I'm just asking
why whata youa hear?
I didn't hear anything
then whata matta?

I give up, here—
take these gloves go

How Long 'Til Summer Holidays?

these self-steering freight car trucks can
be a real pain to change out brake shoes
arching my upper torso
with Gumby-like flexibility
bending over the coal residued sideframe
blindly guiding the brake shoe key
with the experience of a thousand previous

looking up
scanning the adjacent highway
Oh! so wishing I was in that Motorhome
driving down 93 south
going to Radium, Fairmont—wherever
no kids this year

how long 'til summer holidays?

five weeks this year
prime time summer
I can hardly wait
camping, hiking, fishing, golfing
lying in the hammock
hot July sun
bronzing my winter white flesh
no self-steering trucks to curse
no worn brake shoes

Planner to carman working "L" track
"how are you making out on the inspection?"
no cursed Motorola two-way radios

how long 'til summer holidays?

inspecting these never ending
mile and a half long trains
continual mountain grade braking
resulting in an endless series
of badly worn composition brake shoes
must have changed fifty shoes already
running low on shoes and energy
arms numb from the throbbing
still got two more empty trains to inspect
how long 'til summer holidays?

Eye Vision and Hearing Testing

Every year the traveling panel van
loaded with all of the test equipment
pulls up along side the shop
as per Bulletin #36
all employees are reminded
eye vision and hearing tests are required
normally takes about 15 minutes
and your wallet receives yet another card

the regular tester did not show up this year
he was the guy who had all
of the railroad pins on display
willing to trade, sell or buy
now a private contractor performs the tests
first the eye testing
then the hearing tests
back of the van in a cubicle
wearing headphones
you listen for the audio beep
BEEEEP, BEEEP, BEEEP, BEEEP,

same story for the last three tests
he tells me my hearing in one ear is getting worse
“what did you say?”
the hearing in your left year is deteriorating
“I’m sorry what did you say?”
YOUR HEARING!…
stopping in mid sentence
without glancing upwards
he hands me the new updated card

no sense of humor
must be the lonely job
constantly on the road
visiting every railroad location
he is correct though
my hearing is getting worse
maybe it's an occupational illness
nah—just getting older

Then and Only Then

the embodiment of brashness
just bid in from the main shop
eighth, and last term of his apprenticeship
strutting like a fully fanned peacock
knew it all
or so he thought
summoned upstairs by the General Car Foreman
asked what his aspirations might be
pointing with the ardent zeal of a visionary
"to eventually have my feet up on your desk"

waiting patiently on the shop floor
the grizzled old wiry veterans
contentedly smiling to themselves
another one we'll teach him
how to railroad

how to change out coupler components
relying only on the sense of feel
and perplexed facial expressions

how to safely lower a track jack under load
one cog at a time
without losing a hand digit or two

how to water passenger coaches
and not turn into a human icicle
when the mercury slips to minus thirty

how to couple air hoses in the dead of winter

the rubber frozen rock hard

how to re-brass a car on the road

how to—foreign bill
how to—operate an auxiliary crane
how to—interpret the collective agreement

and who knows perchance
after working grave yard shifts
in line points such as
Ignace, Brandon and Revelstoke
he just might return
telling stories of woe
his size ten steel-toed kodiaks
resting comfortably
up on the heavy oak desk

How Can That Be?

His official title was Running Gear Specialist
stationed out of Windsor Station in Montreal
it was the coal cars that periodically brought him out west
one visit alone saw him spend six weeks
testing and monitoring all of the test components
favorite expression was—how can that be?

crawling underneath rail cars
digital calipers in hand
measuring angle of attack
wheel wear
inboard and outboard dimensions
appearance taking on that of a chimney sweeper
we watched in amazement
the once white disposable coveralls
now black with dirt and grease accumulation
how can that be?

inspecting, measuring
gauging and recording
enjoyed his job and all the people he met
be away from home for weeks at a time
never complain
how can that be?

very intelligent yet so humble
his ledger book
showing sketches of little rails cars
data entries
the white pages smeared

from black coal grime
information eventually transformed
into detailed precise reports
colorful charts and graphs
neatly formatted in plasticized binders
how can that be?

the relocation of head office to Calgary took its toll
he remained in Montreal for his family
opted for his severance
now works for a railway supplier
occasionally he does contact us
his role now selling not measuring
white shirt and all
how can that be?

Ode to Fast Eddie

in between periods resting
beads of sweat racing freely down my cheeks
as the oddest name ever to inhabit an arena
the identifiable ZAMBONI
cuts and cleans the ice

one of the bladed competitors
fully attired in the opposition's colors
pokes his head into our crowded dressing room
grabbing my attention as the other players stream out
"did you hear about fast Eddie?" he asks
"yeah he passed away"
yes but did you hear how
yeah still can't believe it
intentional self destruction

stepping onto the ice in tandem
both of us in disbelief
carbon steel skate blades
cutting into the freshly polished ice surface
skating around the traditional warm-up laps
each of us critiquing WHY
shaking our heads in bewilderment

fast Eddie was a railroader through and through
summoned at all hours
like a godsend
he would troubleshoot and repair
those old GM relics
his mere appearance

with crescent wrench in hand
calmed many an exasperated train crew

now he’s gone forever
I always envisioned running into fast Eddie
long after we both retired
reminiscing together
derailments, stalled trains, Bear Creek
no comprehension to this tragedy

thoughts interrupted by the shrill of the whistle
trumpeted by the black and white striped uniform
pointing
face off at center

Regulators

liken to the arrival of the
unexpected taxman
these government inspectors
descend upon the property
tooled with specialty gauges and
well-worn AAR railroad manuals
book pages earmarked for quick reference

Periodic Audits
has it been six months already?

pros in their own right
with minimal disruptions
they carry out the inspections
exceptions noted
defects coded
networking sorted

displaying legitimate frustration
coupled with some over acted innocence
we try to plead our case sheepishly
knowing very well
the inevitable carbon copied forms
will just continue to accumulate
fourteen calendar days
to answer all
highliting
corrections, changes, amendments
taxpayers' dollars hard at work

smiling ever so politely
we wish them farewell
for another six months